The Purpose-Driven Alphabet

A Children's Catechism:
God Tells His Children How to be Joyful

by
Jenny N. Sullivan

ARCHDEACON BOOKS

Published by ARCHDEACON BOOKS
An Imprint of Woody Norman LLC
Hoover, Alabama

Paperback Edition
ISBN-13: 978-0692915622
ISBN-10: 0692915621

For Mia, Ewan, Mae, Ivan, and Anne

And for God's children everywhere

With special thanks to my dear and loving husband, Dan

Who made us? **God made us.**

Who is God? **God is the Supreme Being, infinitely perfect, who made all things and keeps them in existence.**

Why did God make us? **God made us to know, love, and serve Him in this life and to be happy with Him in the next.**

—The Baltimore Catechism

Aa
all

God said, "I will create them *all*,
Big and little, great and small.
Oh yes, I will create them *all*."

"I am the Lord God, who makes all things." Isaiah 44:24

Bb
beginning

So, long ago, in the *beginning*,
God thought, "I'll get this world a-spinning.
That will make a good *beginning*."

"In the beginning, God created the heavens and the earth."
Genesis 1:1

Cc
Creatures

Then God thought, "I'll make some *creatures*,
And I'll give them different features.
How I'll love my little *creatures*."

"You have knit me in my mother's womb." Psalms 139: 13

Dd
divine

He said to them, "My will's *divine*,
Not yours, My dears. Just follow Mine.
My love is in My will *divine*."

"Therefore do not be foolish, but understand what the Lord's will is." Ephesians 5: 17

Ee
everywhere

He said, "You'll find Me *everywhere*,
In flowers, sunshine, quiet prayer.
You can find Me *everywhere*."

"Behind and before you encircle me and rest your hand upon me."
Psalms 139:5

Ff
forever

"I am the great I AM *forever*.
With you always, leaving never.
You can count on Me *forever*."

"God replied, 'I AM who Am.....This is my name forever."
Exodus 3: 14 & 15

Gg
good

And so He tells us to be *good*,
"Please love each other as you should.
You will be joyful when you're *good*."

"Make every effort to add goodness to your faith."
2 Peter 1:5

Hh
heaven

"My saints," He says, "all live in *heaven*.
To them eternal life I've given.
What joy for those who come to *heaven*."

*"Eye has not seen, ear has not heard, and heart has not
guessed what God has prepared for those who love him."*
1 Corinthians 2:9

Ii
incarnation

"I sent My son, the *incarnation*,
Born of flesh for your salvation.
Sent for you and all creation."

"And the word became flesh and dwelt among us."
John 1:14

Jj
Jesus

"I am Lord *Jesus*, My sweet dear.
God the Father sent Me here
So you will know God's always near."

And behold, I am with you always, to the end of the age."
Matthew 28:20

Kk
know

"I want you to serve and *know* Me
And to say 'dear Lord, please show me,
How to let your love o'erflow me.' "

"But grow in grace, and the knowledge of our Lord."
2 Peter 3:18

Ll

love

"I will give you all My *love*
Brought to you from up above.
You, My child, have all My *love*."

"God is love, and whoever abides in love abides in God, and God abides in him." 1 John 4:16

Mm
mercy

"I'll show you *mercy* if you're bad,
Hit your friend or make him sad.
Ask My forgiveness and be glad."

"The Lord your God is a merciful God."
Deuteronomy 4:31

Nn
neighbor

"I command you love your *neighbor*
With your heart and with your labor.
Because I love you, love your *neighbor*."

"You shall love your neighbor as yourself." Matthew 22:39

Oo
omniscient

"I am *omniscient*. I know all.
I see your smiles and tears that fall.
I hear you every time you call."

"Even before a word is on my tongue, Lord, you know it all."
Psalms 139: 4

Pp
pray

"I want My children all to *pray.*
Just tell Me what you have to say.
I'm here for you both night and day."

"This is how you are to pray: Our Father, Who art in Heaven."
Matthew 6:9

Qq
quote

"Read the *Bible*. Pick a *quote*,
That I inspired and writers wrote.
You'll learn about Me from that *quote*."

"Man shall not live by bread alone but by every word that proceeds from the mouth of God." Matthew 4:4

Rr
resurrection

"Another gift, My *resurrection*,
Shows you My divine perfection
And reveals My deep affection."

"I am the resurrection and the life." John 11:25

Ss
spirit

"I'm also Holy *Spirit*, dove,
Tongues of fire from heaven above.
Let Me fill you with My love."

*"There appeared to them tongues as of fire...And they were all
filled with the Holy Spirit."* Acts 2:3-4

Tt
trinity

"We are Holy *Trinity*,
Three in one divinity
Living to infinity."

*God raised this Jesus....He received the promise of the Holy Spirit
and poured it forth." Acts 2: 32 & 33.*

Uu
unity

"We are perfect *unity*,
Father, Son, and Spirit, three.
Share in our community."

*"Teach all nations, baptizing them in the name of the
Father and of the Son and of the Holy Spirit."*
Matthew 28:19

Vv
virtue

"Practice *virtue* every day.
Show My love in every way,
In how you act and what you say."

*"Whatever is true, whatever is honorable, whatever is right,
whatever is pure, whatever is lovely...dwell on these things."*
Philippians 4:8

Ww
wonder

"Enjoy creation's awe and *wonder*,
Tiny worms and giant thunder,
On the earth, above, and under."

"O sing a new song to the Lord, for He has done wonderful things." Psalms 98:1

Xx
exist

"You *exist*, you came to be,
To know and love and follow Me.
Then you'll have joy. Just wait and see.

"In Him we live and move and have our being." Acts 17:28

Yy
Yahweh

"I'm *Yahweh*, Abba, Father, God.
I comfort you with staff and rod
Because I am your loving God."

"Thy rod and thy staff, they comfort me." Psalms 23:4

Zz

zest

"You are salt for others—*zest*.
You are special. You are blessed.
For My sake, always try your best."

"You are the salt of the earth." Matthew 5: 13

"Do everything for the glory of God." 1 Corinthians 10:31

Made in the USA
Middletown, DE
22 September 2019